Wellington
in old picture postcards

by
Douglas Marshall
and
Geoff Heal

European Library - Zaltbommel/Netherlands MCMLXXXIV

GB   ISBN 90 288 2953 9 / CIP

European Library in Zaltbommel/Netherlands publishes among other things the following series:

IN OLD PICTURE POSTCARDS *is a series of books which sets out to show what a particular place looked like and what life was like in Victorian and Edwardian times. A book about virtually every town in the United Kingdom is to be published in this series. By the end of this year about 175 different volumes will have appeared. 1,250 books have already been published devoted to the Netherlands with the title* **In oude ansichten.** *In Germany, Austria and Switzerland 500, 60 and 15 books have been published as* **In alten Ansichten;** *in France by the name* **En cartes postales anciennes** *and in Belgium as* **En cartes postales anciennes** *and/or* **In oude prentkaarten** *150 respectively 400 volumes have been published.*

For further particulars about published or forthcoming books, apply to your bookseller or direct to the publisher.

This edition has been printed and bound by Grafisch Bedrijf De Steigerpoort in Zaltbommel/Netherlands.

INTRODUCTION

The town of Wellington is picturesquely situated in the fertile valley of the River Tone in the south-west of the county of Somerset. The valley is bounded to the north by the Brendon and Quantock Hills, whereas the Blackdown Hills form both the southern boundary of the valley and the Somerset-Devon county border.

The town is first recorded in the early years of the tenth century — as 'Weolingtun' — when it was granted to the Bishop of Sherborne by King Edward the Elder. It subsequently passed to the Bishop of Wells, and 'Walintone' is shown as his property in the Domesday Book of 1086. Wellington became Crown property in the sixteenth century — when its most famous resident was Sir John Popham, whose elaborate tomb can be seen in the parish church. Sir John's offices included Speaker of the House of Commons and Lord Chief Justice of England, and in the latter capacity he presided at the trials of Sir Walter Raleigh and Guy Fawkes.

The town did not figure significantly in the English Civil War, but a number of local men were imprisoned or executed for supporting the Duke of Monmouth at the Battle of Sedgemoor in 1685. The author Daniel Defoe passed through Wellington in 1724, but the town did not again attain national prominence until the distinguished soldier Arthur Wellesley took the title Viscount Wellington of Wellington and Talavera in 1809. Following further victories in the Spanish Peninsular War, Wellesley was elevated through the peerage until he was created Duke of Wellington in 1814, and he is best remembered today for his victory over Napoleon at Waterloo in 1815.

Wellington has been associated with the cloth trade since at least the sixteenth century, and this industry was dominated by the Were family in the eighteenth century and by the Fox family in the following two centuries. The importance of the cloth trade to the town has declined in recent years, but other industries such as bedding manufacture, aerosol production and light engineering have arisen to compensate for this. A brick factory at nearby Poole, which has changed ownership several times since its foundation in 1842, continues to produce bricks from local clay deposits.

Wellington has always benefited from being on the main road between Bristol and Exeter, the two biggest commercial centres in South-West England, and in 1836 the Wellington section of the Grand Western Canal was completed. However, the latter mode of transport was seriously affected by the arrival of the railway in the 1840's, which provided a fast connection between the town and London. Today, however, Wellington has lost its station and is bypassed by much road traffic due to the construction of a relief road and the M5 motorway in the 1970's.

A visitor's first view of Wellington will undoubtedly be the obelisk on the crest of the Blackdown Hills that was erected to commemorate the Duke of Wellington's victory at Waterloo. The town itself has a fine early-sixteenth century parish church and a recently renovated Town Hall of 1833, as well as several other buildings of interest.

During the period covered by this book the population of Wellington remained fairly static at about 6,500, but today (1984) it stands at twice this figure.

All the postcards reproduced in this book are from the authors' collections except the following: 9 and 48, Wellington Museum; 18 and 47, Mr Andrews; 23, Miss Forbear; 31, Mrs Perry; 58, Mrs Richards; and 68, Mrs Palmer.

Anyone requiring more background information on the history of Wellington is recommended to read the following books: G. Allen & R. Bush. *The Book of Wellington.* Buckingham, 1981; A.L. Humphreys. *The History of Wellington.* London, 1889; A.L. Humphreys. *When I was a Boy.* London, 1933.

Parish Church, Wellington.

1. The early-sixteenth century parish church dedicated to St. John the Baptist is situated at the eastern end of the town and is constructed from local ashlar. The south face of the tower has a central stair turret, a feature more typical of Devon churches.

2. This ladies' drapery and hosiery shop in High Street proudly displays the sign WHERE PRICES ARE ALWAYS RIGHT. The premises have changed ownership several times since this photograph was taken and now house an Indian restaurant.

3. A look along Longforth Road when milk and provisions were still delivered by horse-drawn vehicles.

PRIVATE SALOON.

4. The interior of The London Inn, High Street, which was demolished earlier this century. Another postcard proclaims: *Visitors to Wellington are respectfully invited to call and inspect one of the best collections of British coins, medals..., arms and curiosities to be seen in the West of England.*

5. A nearly deserted view of High Street showing a signpost — 'TO ALWAY'S WINE & SPIRIT VAULTS' — standing almost in the middle of the thoroughfare. The ivy-clad frontages on the left add a touch of character to the scene.

6. A large crowd gathers outside the home of 'Judge' Miller in High Street to celebrate Armistice Day, 11 November 1918. Local dignitaries are assembled on the balcony.

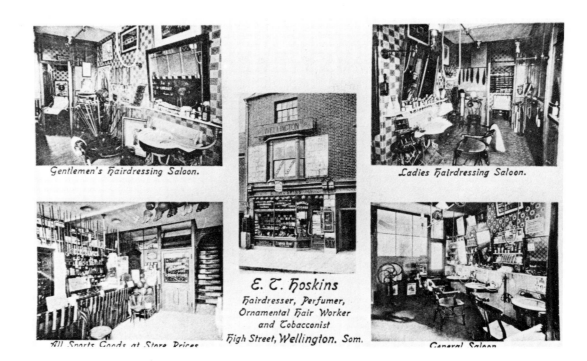

Gentlemen's Hairdressing Saloon.

Ladies Hairdressing Saloon.

E. T. Hoskins

Hairdresser, Perfumer,
Ornamental Hair Worker
and Tobacconist
High Street, Wellington. Som.

All Sports Goods at Store Prices.

General Saloon.

7. This hairdresser had gentlemen's and ladies' saloons (sic.) like the unisex establishments of today, but combined his business with the sale of sports goods.

H. TALBOT, Practical Watchmaker, Jeweller, and Optician. 18, High Street, Wellington, Somerset

8. This postcard demonstrates that even small shopkeepers were keen to advertise both their profession and their wares.

9. The staff of Wellington Post Office pose outside of their place of work in High Street. Mr. Midgley, the postmaster, is seated in the centre and the paternal grandfather of one of the authors (G.J.H.) is fifth from the right in the third row.

10. Procession along High Street in commemoration of the coronation of King George V, June 1911. The horse-drawn engine of the town fire brigade can be seen in the middle distance.

BEATING BOUNDS, MAY. 1914
WELLINGTON. SOM. A

11. A gathering of walkers outside the Town Hall building prior to the 1914 beating of the parish bounds. The young boys in the foreground are carrying willow wands and boundary markers inscribed 'W.P.B. 1914'.

12. The north-west side of the town centre showing (from left to right) the entrance to Cornhill, the Post Office and the Town Hall building. This postcard was therefore issued before the transfer of the Post Office to its present site in High Street in 1911.

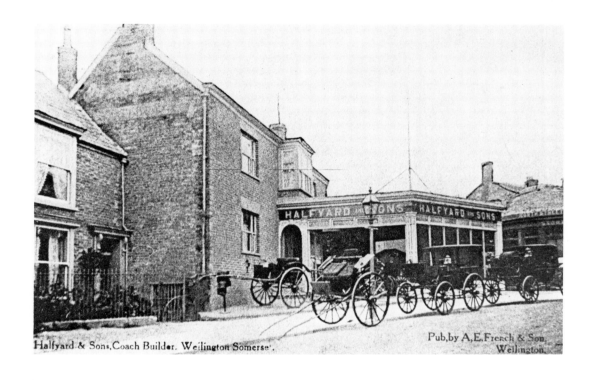

Halfyard & Sons, Coach Builder. Wellington Somerset.

Pub, by A. E. French & Son, Wellington.

13. This postcard was published circa 1906 when horse-drawn transport was slowly being superseded by the motor car. It shows the coach-building workshop of Halfyard & Sons in North Street and was sent by Mr. Halfyard's daughter, Cissie.

14. North Street had more shops in the early 1900's than it has today, and their owners were eager to pose for local photographer A.E. French. The state of the road was not helped by the passage of horses which pulled vehicles full of passengers or goods to the station at the northern end of the town.

15. These butchers have decorated their shop in North Street with holly and mistletoe in preparation for the Christmas trade. This photograph was taken before turkey became the traditional seasonal fare.

16. North Street at its junction with Victoria Street and Courtland Road. The tall railings on the left surround the workhouse which was demolished in 1973, and the large building in the middle distance housed the Co-operative Society until its recent conversion into flats.

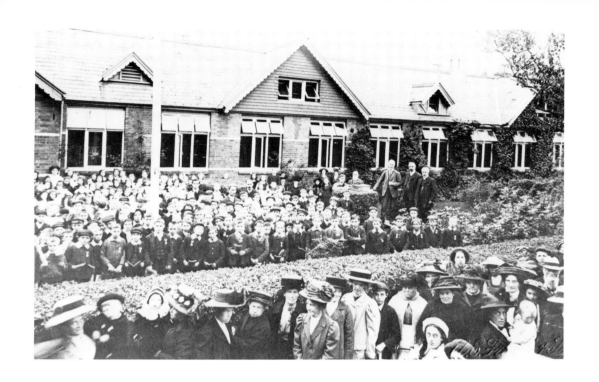

17. Pupils of Courtland Road School assemble for their photograph in 1911. The date, and the fact that they are all wearing medals, suggests that this is another celebration of the coronation of King George V.

18. Uniformed members of Wellington Bicycle Club relax beside their penny-farthings and tricycles at Courtland Road School.

19. The entrance to the Park framing the bandstand. The railings on the right of Beech Grove have long since disappeared.

20. Men in their 'Sunday best' gather around the little wooden bridge over the ornamental pond in the Park.

21. The war memorial in Wellington Park was unveiled on 17 June 1921 to commemorate the dead of the First World War. The number of plaques was later increased to four to include the names of those who fell in the Second World War.

22. Band of Hope members dressed to represent Britannia and the countries of the British Empire. Bands of Hope were run by churches for children between the ages of five and fifteen and these patriotic youngsters probably belonged to the Methodist Church in Waterloo Road.

23. A moment of concentration as members of Wellington Bowling Club measure the distance between the jack and a wood. This photograph was taken in the first decade of this century when the club played at the Athletic Field in Beech Grove.

FLAX WORKERS CAMP WELLINGTON 1918

24. A tented flax workers' camp at the rugby ground in 1918.

25. A Rag Fair was held at the rugby ground in Corams Lane in 1918. The soldier in the foreground of this postcard is probably relaxing after having endured the hardships of the Great War.

26. Springfield, one of the town's smaller streets, remains relatively unchanged from its appearance in this postcard of seventy years ago.

Waterloo Road, Wellington.

27. A view along Waterloo Road from Seymour Street to Corams Lane and Ivy Cottages. The first building on the left is The Dolphin Inn and in the distance can be seen Galpin's Railway Hotel and the Methodist Church.

High Path, Wellington, Somerset

High Path, Wellington, Somerset

28. Waterloo Road and High Path prior to the building of many of the houses on the right-hand side and sixty years before the demolition of Ivy Cottages which can just be seen at the left.

Cornish Riviera Express passing Wellington Station

58019 (JV)

29. A railway station served Wellington from 1844 until its much mourned closure in 1964. This postcard shows one of the Great Western Railway's most famous trains, the Cornish Riviera Express, passing through the station in the first decade of this century.

Tonedale Works, Wellington

30. A view of the extensive textile factory of Fox Bros at Tonedale. This firm developed the distinctive khaki colour and, soon after this photograph was taken, produced thousands of pairs of puttees for the British troops fighting in the Great War.

31. Children outside of Fox Bros factory at Tonedale with their improvised hand-carts.
These carts were used to deliver cloth to outworkers in the town.

32. Whilst workmen leave Fox Bros factory...

33. ...their wives and families wait for them at Crosslands Terrace, Tonedale.

34. An early road accident at the turn of the century. This steam engine has overturned at Burchill's Hill, attracting a crowd of curious onlookers.

35. The first aircraft to visit Wellington landed in a field to the north of the town on 31 May 1912. The French pilot, M. Salmet, was greeted by boys from County School singing 'La Marseillaise'.

36. An idyllic scene beside the River Tone at Winsbier. The cottages still exist in a modified form and the lane on the right leads to Runnington.

B. EVES, AUTHOR

Wellington.

THIS pretty little country town,
  In Somerset doth stand,
With its monuments erected,
  High on the hilly land.

Here tempting shops are well displayed,
  In streets so wide and clean,
With its fine Town Hall and Office,
  So near the centre seen.

How beautiful the green clad Park,
  Where lovers often rove,
Around the shrubs and floral beds,
  And shady old beech grove.

Pinnacled o'er the tall old trees,
  You view the old Church tower,
Oft sweetly chiming on eight bells,
  The peaceful hallowed hour.

The factory makes its woollen serge,
  To clothe you warm and gay,
And o'er the world that you will go,
  You see it worn to-day.

Through Nyne Head's charming, wooded vale,
  Flows on the merry tone,
Where the lively trout are playing,
  Around the river stone.

Away among the Quantock hills,
  Echoes the huntsman's horn,
With the cry of the hounds hard running,
  The fox down in the morn.

Fair Wellington! sweet Wellington,
  Arrayed in Spring with primrose hue,
Where many a homely girl is working,
  And violets blow their scent to you.

[COPYRIGHT

37. A sentimental poem, dated 1919, which extols
the virtues of Wellington. Similar poems were written
for other Somerset towns.

38. The approach to Rockwell Green as it was in about 1910. The Barley Mow Inn can be seen on the right and the skyline is marked by the presence of only one water tower — the second was not built until 1934.

39. A view from the centre of Rockwell Green towards Wellington. The shops on the right are adorned with the colourful enamel signs which were a feature of early-twentieth century advertising.

Wellington, Rockwell Green, All Saints' Church.

40. All Saints Church at Rockwell Green was built in 1889 and consecrated in 1890. It was originally constructed without a tower or spire, but...

7160   ALL SAINTS CHURCH, WELLINGTON SOMERSET.

41. ...these were added in 1908 to give the church its present dignified appearance.

Wellington, Holy Trinity Church.

42. Holy Trinity Church was opened in Mantle Street in 1831 in order to augment the seating of the parish church. However, the church fell into disuse in just over a hundred years and was finally demolished in 1966.

The Almshouses   Wellington, Somerset

43. A postcard, based on a photograph taken at the end of the last century, which shows Sir John Popham's Almshouses in Mantle Street. These were rebuilt in 1833 and became the Roman Catholic Church of St John Fisher in 1940.

44. One of the many small family shops — in this case a butcher's shop in Mantle Street — which have characterised country towns throughout this century. The proprietor and his family stand proudly outside the premises which today are a do-it-yourself shop.

45. A peaceful scene in Mantle Street where a small group, including a donkey cart, has stopped to pose for the photographer.

Mantle Street, Wellington.

46. Mantle Street leading to the south-western end of the town. This postcard served as a subtle form of advertising because it was published by J. Quick who owned the store on the left.

47. A group of revellers assembles outside The Three Cups Hotel in Fore Street to celebrate the Relief of Mafeking in 1900. The flags above the arch bear the portraits of the military leaders of the Boer War.

48. The custom of 'firing the anvils' is performed in the cattle market between Fore Street and North Street, on 22 June 1911, to start the celebrations of the coronation of King George V. The cattle market is now the site of North Street car park.

49. A coach and pair hurries along Fore Street, but the changing times are heralded by the presence of a garage and the 'Automobile Association' sign hanging outside The Squirrel Hotel.

SQUIRREL HOTEL, Wellington, SOMERSET.

First-Class Family and Commercial Hotel.   Headquarters of Cyclists' Touring Club.
Posting in all its branches.   Hearse and Funeral Coaches on the Premises.   M. CHIPLING. Proprietor.

50. An advertising postcard for The Squirrel Hotel, Fore Street. Part of the building became the premises of the Wellington Museum in 1983 after having lain empty for several years.

51. Rowe Bros emporium in Fore Street. The message on the reverse reads 'We had 5,000 (of these cards) printed for an add. (sic.) for the Sale but they did not come in time'.

52. A view of Fore Street which shows the shop of W.H. Smith & Son several buildings west of its present location. This firm published several series of Wellington postcards from 1907 onwards, examples of which appear as Nos. 3, 41 and 73 in this book.

53. A view along Fore Street from the centre of the town. The two large awnings on the left advertise the businesses of Peel Bros, tailors/outfitters, and Shaplands, bakers/caterers/confectioners/restaurateurs.

54. An animated town centre scene during the 1908 Agricultural Show. Temporary stalls have been erected outside the Town Hall building on the left and a horse-bus can be seen carrying visitors from the station.

55. South Street seen from the town centre. The awnings supported by vertical iron rods indicate a hot summer day although there are not many shoppers about.

56. The Wellington Town Band leads a procession along South Street on Lifeboat Saturday in 1908. A series of postcards illustrates the progress of the procession to The Basins where a lifeboat was launched. Money was collected throughout to aid the Royal National Lifeboat Institution.

57. In 1908 Wellington was the venue for an agricultural show, and decorated arches were constructed at the entrances to the town in Fore Street, High Street, South Street and Station Road. This postcard shows the arch in South Street.

58. A red deer stag is displayed outside The Green Dragon Inn in South Street. It has probably just been brought down from the Blackdown Hills.

59. Laying the foundation stone to the extension of the Sunday School buildings at South Street Baptist Church in 1907.

The Salvation Army Band, Wellington, Somerset.

60. The Salvation Army has been based at Scotts Lane since the end of the nineteenth century, and this postcard shows that it possessed a fine band as early as 1914.

61. Wellington Cottage Hospital was built in 1891 thanks to the benevolence of Mr. Egerton Burnett and continues to provide an invaluable service to this day.

62. A view of South Street showing the imposing building that was the warehouse of Egerton Burnett, a world-renowned cloth manufacturer. The building still bears the royal coat of arms but is now part of Wellington School.

63. An Egerton Burnett's advertising postcard of the 1920's showing the extent of this company's trading in Europe. The card was sent to a customer in Marostica, north-eastern Italy.

64. Some of the buildings of County School in South Street, showing (from left to right) the school room, headmaster's house and chemistry laboratories. The two bystanders are probably school employees.

65. A group of schoolboys seated outside the cricket pavilion at West Somerset County School, now Wellington School. This card was sent by the Chairman of the school's Old Boys Committee.

66. A quiet scene at the top of South Street showing The Sanford Arms public house and a small confectioner's premises which, for many years, was the tuck-shop for pupils at Wellington School.

67. Blackdown School was one of a number of small private schools that flourished in the town during the first quarter of this century. Situated in Wellesley Park, the house now serves as a home for the elderly.

68. A tranquil rural scene close to the water tower in Dark Lane. This land has now been used for housing development.

69. A gamekeeper outside his cottage just below Wellington Monument. Behind him are his dog and, suspended from a line, a number of creatures killed in the course of his work.

70. Wellington Monument, a celebration of the first Duke of Wellington's victory at Waterloo, overlooks the town to the north. Its construction commenced in 1817, but it did not reach its present height of 175 feet until 1892. Four cannon stood around the monument between 1911 and the early 1940's and a flight of 235 steps lead to a viewing chamber.

A Souvenir of Wellington!

71. A composite postcard that showed the purchaser which other cards were available in the series. They range from the ubiquitous view of the parish church to a scene at the railway station.

72. Time for a rest during the 1914 beating of the parish bounds. A boy raises the union flag whilst other walkers take the opportunity to quench their thirsts.

STUDHOLME BRIDGE. NEAR WELLINGTON. SOMERSET

73. The iron bridge which crossed the Grand Western Canal to the north of the town. Although this stretch of the canal has now been filled in, the dismantled bridge can still be found close to its original site. The bridge was erected in 1869 at a cost of $12.

Old Canal Bridge, Nynehead Park, Wellington, Somerset.

74. The aqueaduct between Wellington and Nynehead which carried the Grand Western Canal.

NYNEHEAD CHURCH, WELLINGTON. SOM

75. The picturesque church of All Saints at Nynehead, parts of which date from the thirteenth century. The church is famous for its stained glass and its Italian Renaissance sculpture.

The "Beauties" of WELLINGTON cannot be exaggerated. Too busy to write.

76. A very appropriate postcard with which to conclude this brief look at Wellington in the early years of this century.